Terms and Conditions

LEGAL NOTICE

The Publisher has strived to be as accurate and complete as possible in the creation of this report, notwithstanding the fact that he does not warrant or represent at any time that the contents within are accurate due to the rapidly changing nature of the Internet.

While all attempts have been made to verify information provided in this publication, the Publisher assumes no responsibility for errors, omissions, or contrary interpretation of the subject matter herein. Any perceived slights of specific persons, peoples, or organizations are unintentional.

In practical advice books, like anything else in life, there are no guarantees of income made. Readers are cautioned to reply on their own judgment about their individual circumstances to act accordingly.

This book is not intended for use as a source of legal, business, accounting or financial advice. All readers are advised to seek services of competent professionals in legal, business, accounting and finance fields.

You are encouraged to print this book for easy reading.

Table Of Contents

Foreword

Chapter 1:
The Benefits Of Video Products

Chapter 2:
Choosing Your Topic For Your Product

Chapter 3:
Prepare An Outline And Script

Chapter 4:
The Tools

Chapter 5:
Getting Sales

Chapter 6:
Final Tips

Wrapping Up

Foreword

Here's a not-so-secret mystery: the market is getting sick of the common eBooks and special reports that assures the most revolutionary info. They require something fresh... something additional... something that they may actually react to. And it has become a marketer's challenge to get hold of novel products that would shake up a market slowly passing into apathetic stupefaction.

And the most prosperous product types that have been devised in recent months are video products. Yep, video that you may actually watch from your monitor. Video that's accompanied with audio comments, which try to inform, if not to entertain as well.

How To Create A Video Product To Sell For Clickbank

Chapter 1:
The Benefits Of Video Products

Synopsis

Video products provide a lot of advantages over conventional text products. Studies have demonstrated that:

- Individuals would like to watch and listen to videos instead of read
- Videos typically convert better than conventional written material.
- Videos may be viral in nature, and they may be hosted free of charge on net video streaming sites like YouTube or MetaCafe. As an alternative, you are able to likewise host your videos on your own domain if your server may handle it and your provider allows those file types.
- Additionally, with the emergence of social media networking sites like Facebook and Twitter, you are able to provide video samples or video reviews of your product, and they've the power to go viral (circulate by word of mouth).

If you are able to capitalize on this phenomenon, your marketing campaign and product will grow exponentially.

Videos have allowed the big dogs in the industry to establish a deeper connection with their customers and dramatically better the results of their web and product campaign.

The Benefits

Yes, there are a lot of reasons why video products are better than penned works, which have gotten to be old-hat after a decade more or less.

- Individuals react more to what they may see and hear, instead of what they may merely read.
- Individuals are more stirred up with what they get to enjoy viewing.
- Some info which can't be clearly expressed with composed works may in reality be demonstrated with video demonstrations.
- Video presentations deliver info in a clearer, and often, more concise fashion.
- Video presentations are regarded as more professional products equated to their counterparts.

Indeed, video products are easily better choices compared to conventional assortments. However the issue that most marketers go through with this medium is the apparently complicated process involved in their production. This, all the same, shouldn't be the case. With the correct knowledge on how to go forward, you'd realize the producing a video product is easy.

Video Ads

Video ads are the future of net advertising. The video benefits and disfavors point to a strong future with the mass medium in the ad world. As a matter of fact, net video advertising is projected to grow at an amazing rate!

What is video advertisement?

Net video advertising is cropping up all over the Net. As more and more individuals are becoming connected to the Net thru broadband connections, the disadvantages of slow load speeds are no more a major worry with net advertisers.

Video ads are advertising that integrate streaming video. Streaming banners are an illustration of video ads. With this sort of ad, the video is confined inside the boundaries of the banner ad, which is great because it may run without hindering the user from seeing the remainder of the site. Streaming video in the body of an e-mail is another popular form of video ad.

What do video ads commonly contain? Consider it like a miniature television commercial. It may include a manifestation of a product, a testimonial about its effectiveness, or apply a clever "plot" to accomplish better "branding" or recognition for the material in question. Net video ads are likewise quite popular with political candidates and for exhibiting movie previews or "trailers."

While this is a newer venue of net advertising, it's developing steadily. Statistics project that the sum of money spent on net video ads will achieve $657 million in the near future. The growth stems from the flourishing popularity of broadband connections.

Learning With Video

Multimedia is a word often heard and discussed among educational technologists nowadays. Unless distinctly defined, the word may alternately mean a sensible mix of assorted mass media like print, audio and video.

Or it might mean the development of computer-based hardware and software produced on a mass scale and all the same allows individualized utilization and learning. Basically, multimedia blends multiple levels of learning into an educational tool that allows for variety in courses of study presentation.

Today's multimedia is a cautiously woven compounding of text, graphic art, sound, animation, and video factors. When you let an end user, i.e. the viewer of a multimedia project, control 'what' and 'when' and 'how' of the factors that are delivered and presented, it gets to be interactive multimedia.

Besides being a mighty tool for making presentations, multimedia provides unique benefits in the field of education. For example, text alone merely doesn't allow for a "feel" of any of Shakespeare's plays.

In instructing biology, a teacher can't make a killer whale awaken in a classroom. Multimedia enables us to supply a way by which learners may experience their subject in a vicarious fashion. The key to furnishing this experience is having co-occurring graphic, video and audio. The appeal of multimedia learning is better illustrated by the fame of the video games presently available in the market.

These are multimedia programs blending text, audio, video, and animated graphics in an easy-to-use manner.

Similarly, you can use a multimedia product to prepare or to update information or to teach so as to inspire and also add insight to a lesson, thereby bettering the quality of the course. The uses of multimedia need not be seen as a tool for courses only. In industries people need to be trained. Training may take place individually at the learner's pace and on his/her own time.

The cognitive advantages of interactive videos:

In contrast to their traditional, non-interactive opposites, interactive dynamic visual images let users adapt their form and material to their individual cognitive skills and requirements.

Interactive videos lead to more effective forms of learning. This belief was tested in an observational study, where participants learned to tie 4 marine knots of different complexness by watching either non-interactive or interactive videos.

The outcomes demonstrate that in the interactive circumstance, participants utilized the interactive features like stopping, replaying, reversing or altering speed to adjust the pace of the video demonstration. This led to a spotty distribution of their attention and cognitive resources across the videos, which was more marked for the hard knots. Therefore users of non-interactive presentations required substantially more time than users of the interactive videos to get the necessary skills for tying the knots.

Chapter 2:

Choosing Your Topic For Your Product

Synopsis

Pick out a matter you wish to tackle, preferably a subject you're already acquainted with.

The First Steps

Choosing a video subject has forever been an intriguing subject.

There are a lot of variables and conditions, so many matters to think about that most individuals get confused and surrender before they ever get cracking.

There are a few details which may lead us on to discovering the solution. Potential video product authors need to think about these points and utilize them as indicators to help them pick out a worthwhile subject.

Never produce a product about something that has no resale worth.

It's a totally pointless exercise; if the likely buyers are not there the sales won't be either. Do your preparation; utilize Google and /or other Search Engines to research keywords that are popular.

The search results will show if the keyword (subject) is popular and meriting of additional research. For example, search for something like "How to get rid of Spiders "and you'll see that there are a lot of search results, which you might have thought that there would not be.

Attempt the search term 'Tennis' though and you'll discover that there are many more, millions as a matter of fact. Great search terms commonly go hand in hand with popular subjects, though not always.

I understand what's going through your brain now, how do I contend in this area?

Well, Search Engines merely indicate how many product pages are available for a certain search term. Attempt to find a few good search terms on Google for your decided subject and make a note of them.

Google Alerts

Research is all-important in discovering a profitable niche for your particular concern or video as well as in promoting it. Among the best free research tools I've discovered is Google Alerts.

Google Alerts will search for you. When you sign up, you'll pick out a query or topic. Then you'll receive "alerts" thru email updates of the cutting-edge relevant Google results (sites, news, etc.) based on your selection.

Although you are able to use Google Alerts to do a lot of types of research like monitoring a developing news story, keeping current on a rival or industry, becoming notified if and when other people are discussing you or your product, and keeping tabs on your name and reputation, it may likewise be used to discover information on areas where many individuals have an interest, troubles or questions.

Once you're ready to go in Google Alerts, simply enter in the subjects (you are able to sign up for as many search terms as you want) you've been thinking about producing a video on and schedule how frequently you wish to be notified. That may be weekly, daily or as the news is breaking.

You are able to do a comprehensive search or you are able to specify it further and only be alerted from particular blogs, web, video or groups. You'll soon get a great sense of what info is out there already on the subject and if you are able to add something fresh to the niche.

For instance, you might be interested in doing a cooking video series on vegetarian sweets. You sign up to be alerted to the terms "vegetarian sweets" and see there are a lot of individuals talking about it. Then you are able to click on the site links provided to get a better sense of the buzz around the subject and what sort of info is already out there.

You might likewise discover that there is not much action around that question. That gives you great info as well. Perhaps this topic or niche isn't as hot of an area you thought it might be and now you are able to decide if your time and effort producing a video would be better expended in a different way.

You might likewise discover really similar videos or products like yours are offered. Once again, this gives you a great indication of the sort of competition you face. If you're still excited about this subject, then you have to position yourself differently and decide what unparalleled angle you're bringing to the market.

Clickbank

Our next step is to utilize Clickbank. Their procedure works like this– Producers of original products list their products on Clickbank and aspiring Affiliate marketers take the products and market them for a fee chosen by the product maker. Commonly anything from 50% and up.

Both the product creators and the affiliates profit from this agreement.

The web site likewise serves our purpose as we may search the Clickbank market to help us with our research.

Log into Clickbank.com and go to the Marketplace, you don't have to be a member. Take your selected keywords or phrases in turn and put them into the search box, you are able to utilize "" to surround your search terms to cut back on the number of unrelated terms if you want.

By the bye, you are able to likewise do this in the Search Engine search box also. Once the results come up take particular note of the 'Grav' terms at the bottom of every entry, these show how well the product is doing, any 'Grav' at 10 or over signals that the product is doing alright indeed.

Sales Page

Once you discover a relevant product here, make a few notes on the keywords and likewise take a look at the Sales page, remember you have to compose a sales page for your product at some stage and you are able to learn a lot by taking a peek at other sales pages that are hading best.

You are able to copy the sales pages to your disc drive and view them later if need be.

Sales pages are an indicant of how well the product sells, a great product with a poor sales page won't sell as well as a poor product with a great sales page but that's a different story.

Chapter 3:
Prepare An Outline And Script

Synopsis

The videos we watch all beginning with a script, but prior to the script ever being written, a few authors make an outline. An outline may take a lot of forms, from a simple index card format of scenes to an elaborate step outline that gives an overview of the video.

A few writers outline with a pen and paper and other people utilize software particular to the task. The level to which a writer outlines depends on individual authors and their work habits. Whichever technique you use, constructing an outline may make help you tell your story more expeditiously.

Can you become a great video scriptwriter? I think the answer is yes. As a communicator, you are able to make the shift from writing books, procedures, and pamphlets to authoring video scripts utilized in training, recruiting, and marketing.

The Video Beginnings

Choose how you wish to outline. The index card technique has been around for years. It's easy and effective as you are able to keep your outline in front of you all the time. If you have a cork board that is useable, you are able to pin your index cards to the cork board and rearrange them as you set up your outline.

There are in addition to that, software programs available, like Movie Outline, aimed at making the outline procedure simpler. If you utilize screenwriting software like Final Draft or Movie Magic Screenwriter, these platforms have outline tools inbuilt. Irrespective of the technique you pick out, the process of outlining stays the same.

Choose whether you wish to do a scene draft or a step draft. A scene draft is much less elaborate. Write a scene head on the face of your index card, at the top. Compose the heading as you would in your script. For instance, Beach-Daylight. Below the scene head, write an overview of the view.

The overview ought to be a short description of the activity that takes place in the view, affecting any major point. Likewise include a notation about anything in the scene that has to occur to set up a different scene in the video. Turn the card over and put the names of the characters or pictures that appear in the scene. Include any mentions about character or picture demeanor in this section also.

Enlarge your scene outline by stapling additional index cards to the chief scene cards they associate to. During the course of authoring a video, you'll need to cross-index scenes, or even small actions inside a scene, to additional scenes in the video.

These are events that have to happen to ensure a different scene or action in the video adds up. Compose these actions individually and attach them to the scene index card in which they occur, and then indicate the scene you wish to relate the info to in a parenthetic note. This lets you track the continuity of your story. These individual steps ought to be more detailed than the principal scene card. Put down precisely what the characters do and how it associates with the referenced scene.

Put your cards under a general three-act structure to help you pace your video. The three-act structure is the most basic structure utilized for the movies. A 2 hour video is about 120 pages. The first thirty pages is act one, the middle sixty are act 2, and the concluding thirty make up the 3rd act. Hang a three-act timeline on your cork board and pin your scene cards below the act they fall under to help you ascertain whether or not your scenes happen where they ought to in the overall structure of the script. Your video may not be 2 hours long, nut you get the picture.

The Script

For a technical communicator, arriving at the switch from a print medium to a visual one may be a very jolty ride. People accustomed to churning out e-zines and brochures frequently approach the video script the same way--as words instanced by pictures. Unlike the flat print world, video provides a writer a dynamic, multi-dimensional palette-- movement, viewpoint, sound effects, music, character, dialogue, and narration--even hush.

We are discussing scriptwriting for business video, not for scriptwriting sequels to blockbuster movies. However scripts utilized for business and education videos have gotten to be as sophisticated as those for television and films, and they carry the extra requirement of conveying particular content.

So how do you become a scriptwriter? You have to first get a "basic knowledge of production strategies and terminology." You have to grasp an understanding of what you are able to and not do with a video camera and with software.

If you view home videos, I trust you already are acquainted with production strategies. Because of home video, we comprehend more today than ever before about the ways and means of the video industry, its cultural influence, its art form, and its applied science.
Not only are we movie lovers, but in a confined way, we're likewise students and critics of this medium. Our DVD players let us rewind for repeated viewings, view particular scenes, study the editing and camera work, and even make out production flubs.

This shift from a print to a visual medium likewise calls for your acquisition of a few new skills. You must become acquainted with visualization, dialogue, timing, and budget restraints.

For many, visualization is among the hardest skills related to scriptwriting. The power to see the pictures the words evoke and to view those pictures as active, rather than static, is a skill that requires time to cultivate. You have to learn to let the video speak rather than the words.

You'll attempt to tell a creative visual story with impact and style blending audio, video, music, and graphics. How you tell that story depends a great deal on the cash and resources available for. Animation, special effects, multiple locations, and big-name talent will add energy to your video only when you can afford it.

- You have to be able to pinpoint the needs of your target audience and separate crucial from unneeded info.
- You must be able to organize info into coherent sequences.
- You must be skilled to tune into audience attitudes, motivations, learning styles, and interests.
- You must be able to present info and convey ideas with pictures, not simply words.
- Creative thinking is called for successful scripts.

There are numerous basic questions that you need to ask yourself about the video:

- What is this video supposed to achieve?
- Who's my target audience?
- When and where will the video be shown?
- What info do I include, and how do I need to present it?
- What are the available resources and budget?
- With whom will I work on this?
- What is the deadline?

Do your research and gather all the background info you think you'll need. Understand the audience's perceptions and attitudes.

Select what concepts you'll utilize to grab (the hook) and hold your audience's attention. Here are a few concepts:

- Speaking head. One individual on camera delivers a straightforward demonstration. The camera sometimes cuts to simple visuals like charts, lists, or graphs.
- Ad-lib interview. One individual equipped with points to cover or questions interviews an authority on the topic.
- Arranged interview. Both participants have scripted parts. The interviewer asks organized questions, and the interviewee reacts with prepared answers.

- Documentary. A narrator, commonly off camera, takes the audience on an optic tour, reporting on the program topic.
- Voice-over narration. Visuals are accompanied by narration from somebody off camera. The narrator might describe a job procedure being exhibited or might comment on other sorts of visuals.
- Demonstration. The individual on camera describes while demonstrating.
- Dramatization. Actors play roles in a written story.
- Animation. Cartoon characters supply instruction.

Whatever you do, be sure to present the materials in a way that will hold the attention and interest of your audience. You are able to do this by:

- Engaging the audience's emotions
- Presenting your ideas in fresh, succinct, clear, and originative ways
- Making your viewers care about the content
- Utilizing aural and visual variety

While visualizing your scenes, if you discover spots that don't seem as though they'd hold viewer attention, make alterations.

Remember, if you lose your audience, you've compromised the entire purpose of your effort.

Chapter 4:
The Tools

Synopsis

Let's have a look at a few of the tools you require for your video production. The most crucial thing is plainly the camera. The caliber of the picture comes from the camera.

Choose a camera that not simply fits your budget, but likewise yields the highest caliber that you're seeking. Nowadays it's a lot more puzzling as you have dv, hdv, and then you've hd cameras altogether. Choose them wisely and likewise think about the future of where video is going, which is largely hd. When you already have a camera, then there is no excuse for you not to understand everything about it.

What You Need

Your PC is the element of introducing the video and editing. Again, the most crucial thing is, get a PC that you may afford and that has comparatively high speed. Truly the number 1 thing that you need to save your cash for when you purchase your PC is ram.

Acquire as much ram as you may afford. That's essential for manipulation of those large video files. A different thing you may wish to consider, if you purchase your PC at another point, maybe down the road, is to purchase an external disc drive to store your videos. The reason is, video files are really big.

That's number 1. But truly, number 2 is, you don't wish your video files on the same disc drive that your operating system is on. It has an inclination to have stutter steps and matters that occur once you edit as your video is on the same disc drive that your operating system is on. Think about, at some point, buying an external disc drive to do your video editing.

Absolutely invest in some sort of a lighting kit. Digital video is really unforgiving, exceedingly unforgiving, with dark scenarios. Among the reasons is it can't truly tell the difference between dark grays and blacks. So if you get into a dark room everything looks sort of mawkish. Or if it's not lit advantageously.

Truly, among the best points I may give you, when we get to the section on lighting we'll talk a bit more, is to comprehend that great digital video truly depends a lot on great lighting and naturally you the operator. A tripod is a must. If you're going to shoot any sort of video, purchase a tripod. It doesn't mean you have to eliminate the

hand-held scenario; however the most crucial thing is you need to have a firm shot. Regardless how steady your hand is, it's better to use a tripod. Those are a few things. Likewise real quick, audio wise, constantly monitor it.

Let's talk about audio.

Lucas stated it best "50% of the video experience is sound." Most videographers neglect sound. They take it for granted. Most importantly, you wish to monitor your audio when you're recording. Even if it's an inexpensive pair of headphones, it doesn't matter. Constantly monitor it.

The 2nd thing you wish to comprehend is, on your camera, what sort of microphone do you have? There are particular patterns on microphones that you have to comprehend. Make certain you comprehend how your audio is being recorded on your camera. One matter to recall about digital video and audio is it's really unforgiving if the levels are too hot.

Many cameras, particularly professional, have meters that demonstrate the levels of the audio. Monitor those and listen really cautiously. You don't wish them to peak at zero. If you acquire distorted audio, there's nearly no way to do away with it at all in editing. Likewise to consider an extra microphone. It's really crucial to invest in different caliber microphones for what you're doing.

Lighting.

We've been speaking a lot about how to make your videos appear professional. Now, we're going to discuss lighting. Let me state

something about digital video as a whole. It's really, very important that you pay attention to lighting. Particularly low light levels. They don't do really well.

Even a few of the things you've seen in theaters, a few of these digital videos, particularly Star Wars, which was among the first digital videos shot in all digital format, they still, if you look close, have troubles with lighting.

I believe I mentioned before, when you've dark levels of black and grays, it makes the camera work harder to work out what it's viewing. Keep a truly, truly close look at your lighting and your exposure levels. That implies yes, you'll have to invest in a lighting kit of some type if you haven't already. You don't have to drop a lot of cash. Essentially you may choose whatever sort of lights you wish.

If you're shooting someone, you never point the light flat at them. You commonly point it up, so it's not so hard, the shadows aren't hard, you ought to avoid shadows anyhow.

Among the best things to do when you're shooting inside is to utilize a single light, if its ultra- bright, and simply bounce the light off the ceiling. Is a single light that's pointed up at the ceiling and that diffuses the light as the ceiling is white, and provides it a nice glow.

If you do it with one light great, but 2 lights is better and truly nice professional quality you utilize 3 lights. You utilize one as the main, the fill, and occasionally a spot. Essentially, that's it with lighting but there's one additional issue. If you can't afford these that's ok. I'd still advise you to invest in some sort of lighting. Perhaps you may buy the sort of light that sits on top of your camcorder. Constantly pay

attention to your lighting cause it's the most crucial part of digital video.

Following, let's consider how all this works with your PC.

We're now putting video into the PC. We have to talk about organizing your clips as now we're escaping from tangible holding your a camera and shooting to the virtual world. You have to be moderately organized in digital video.

That entails organizing your clips. Basically, once you begin importing your clips, in some sort of program, I Movie or windows movie maker for example, you may see there's a place where the clips are stored. Commonly in most programs it's named the bin.

Adobe Premier, Final Cut Pro, even Advent all have a region where your clips are stored. In other programs they have folders where you may put clips in. Audio clips, graphics, all those sort of things that make your life simpler.

Once your clips are prepared, you may then bring them down into what the area is named the time line. The time line is truly where you begin to tell your story. That's truly the space where you do all the core editing and make transitions. From here, now your originative powers are released as all you have to do is coordinate and tell the story that you set up through your outline and or script.

The following thing we're going to discuss are graphics and titles and essentially how to do that to make your video jump out at people.

Now that you've coordinated your clips and you've got your story all set up, it's time to look into graphics and titles. I'm going to provide you a few pointers around graphics and titles. Keep them simple.

Likewise remember, they're simply there for one reason if you have been shooting video with your camera, to augment your video. If your graphics and titles are competing with your video, you might wish to reconsider what you're doing.

Titles are very crucial and there's one thing I wish to give you that's a nice little tip. Once you utilize white fonts on a black background it makes the text look 10 percent larger than really is. That is why a lot of movie promos utilize white text on a black background. It simply gives that illusion that it's bigger.

Likewise, a different thing you wish to try to stay away from are colorful fonts, like red, green, and blue. They have a disposition, on particular TVs or screens, to tear or bleed. Attempt to avoid those.

Keep your fonts big and crisp. Attempt not to place too many words on one line and have fun with it. It's truly quite simple. In that program that you were utilizing here, you may simply go ahead and play with another font, animations and see what works better for you. Be cautious.

This is among the things you wish to set up after your story is assembled in a video format wise. Put differently, a few individuals jump to the titles and they spend so much time on the titles that they really don't get to the video that has to be edited. Edit your video initially, add the titles second, goes a long way.

Be it just pictures or graphics, the approach remains the same. Your editing software likewise allows you to get images that appear on the screen for a limited duration. Import your pictures and music in the editing software.

- Import your pictures, your music, in the editing software,
- Put your music on the "time-line" (time line)
- Place your pictures in the order of your chosen scenario.
- A final viewing window lets you view your mounting rapidly underway.
- Add your transitions opening (top), closure (end), and the transitions that will let you connect all your clips.
- Watch the result in the viewing window.
- The duration of your video from images ought to match the duration of the music you pick out.
- If you're satisfied with the result, you have to export the assembly carried out in a single file video / audio.
- The export will be in the format of your choice (. Avi,. Mpg,. Wmv) after appointing this file.

Rendering

We're almost at the end here of making your pro looking video -- But there's a thing called rendering. Rendering is a procedure of once you've lined up your clips, titles and everything, your audio and have edited it -- is the process of telling your PC that now this is the format I have to go to.

Whether you're going to the web, DVD... you have to render. Tell the PC to make that video that certain size and data format that you have to kick it out to.

Let me back up a little. You have to comprehend that in digital video, we have the ability to output in any way we wish to. We may place it on the web, stream it, make DVD's of it; we may do all sorts of stuff. We may even export it back out to our cameras to demonstrate it if we need to. So, rendering is truly specific on your PC.

The quicker your computer, the quicker your rendering time. That goes back to -- if you're in the market for a PC, attempt to find the quickest PC your money may buy. If not, it's all right. It simply means you might have a long dinner while your PC is rendering out the video segment.

Codecs

There's one thing I wish to share with you. It's what we call 'codecs'. Codecs is short for compression-decompression. You have to recall this is digital video and your video is being compressed. When you bring that video into your PC you've the option to set up additional codecs. For instance, let's suppose you wish to go to an .avi format. That is a codec. It's simply a different way it's compressed.

You physically have to tell the PC "I'm going from this format to this format." That likewise couples with rendering, because as soon as you shift formats, guess what? Your rendering time climbs up. Suppose for instance, I wish to send to a DVD. I tell it to export to DVD.

Remember, it's changing its codec. It's changing the way it's compressed. Digital video to DVD, which is mpeg2.

There are virtually hundreds of compression strategies out there. There's mPEG2, mpeg4, flash video, which are all sorts of compression. The thing you have to know to keep your videos professional is the way you could give it to other people.

Suppose, for instance, again I need this video to be placed on the web. When you actually export or render it, you're actually going to choose the codec that represents your medium.

I won't go into a lot of detail here, but there's adequate info on the web and books out there that will help you clearly recognize the format you need that will be for DVD, HD, the web, iPods, you name it.

The most crucial thing I may stress is, learn everything you can about your camera and editing programs. Likewise remember digital video is wholly dependent on excellent lighting, so don't hesitate to get a few lights and light your scene well.

Remember composition, it's truly crucial. Move things around, move individuals around to get the scene looking precisely the way you need it.

And audio, I cannot stress enough. Monitor your audio once you're recording, make certain you have some good mics. And one thing I didn't tell you about audio is, prevent the bath syndrome. What does that imply?

Many individuals utilize their camera microphone, and they're too far away from the subject and they're in a room that bounces sound, essentially the audio goes all over the place. And the mic essentially

isn't close enough, to the source, and so it sounds like you're in the bath. If that's occurring, get an external mic.

There's so much to digital video that we have not covered, but you should not be discouraged. This is a great starting point for you to dive in. My goal truly is to get you motivated, to go for it.

Remember, it's an art form; it's not simply fun, it's an art form, and that means you put a little time into it.

Chapter 5:
Getting Sales

Synopsis

If you'd like to sell a video product, you'll have to connect with your target audience. A lot of individuals turn to the Internet in search of info, and a video may help them to see things in action. You are able to sell online videos on a variety of topics--from craft projects to job advice. Produce a sales page that captures the customer's attention and encourages them to purchase. Make certain your video is inaccessible to those who haven't paid for it as well.

Getting People Interested

Understand your target buyer. Your customer ought to have a problem he or she needs to resolve, and the solution ought to be in your video. Knowing the sort of buyer you have will help you to produce a sales page that's more in line with what that individual will want. For instance, the design and wording for a teenager might be bright and colorful; utilizing a lot of slang, but the design and wording for men in their 40s might be more subtle and sophisticated.

Envisage one prototype individual who's your main buyer. Give him or her a name, an age, a line of work. Does he or she have a family? If so, how many youngsters does he have? Where does she live? What are her interests? Does she have training? Put down the attributes of your prototype buyer. When advertising and marketing, keep the buyer you produced in mind.

Utilize Free Word Tracker or other keyword tools to discover the keywords your target audience is searching for. Net marketing is crucial. It doesn't make sense to have a web page and not utilize the key phrases your potential buyers are looking for. Bear in mind that most individuals search short 2 to 3 word phrases.

Network and research to discover your target audience. Ask your acquaintances and relatives what things they'd look for if they were your likely buyers. Discover net forums that talk about your product. Research what your rivals are doing. Stay on top of what your industry hum is about for successful target marketing.

Think about outsourcing some of your marketing to discover your target audience. It's easier than ever to discover qualified and

knowledgeable experts for fair rates to produce marketing strategies for your company's target audience.

Don't quit researching your target audience. Your marketing technique must keep pace with change.

List Benefits and Info

List the advantages of your video product. The advantages of your product ought to answer the question, "What's in it for me?" for your buyer. Be cautious you don't list the features of your video but the ways the buyer will benefit once they watch your videos. For instance, a benefit of having a video product as opposed to a live presentation is convenience

Product info may persuade consumers to buy the product. The product has to fulfill a need or solve an issue that the buyer might be experiencing. For instance, if a buyer requires a digital camera for a night wedding, she will seek a camera that successfully executes at night. Consequently, product developers must make it a priority to give accurate product data buyers may depend on.

Supply a product overview for the reader including the name of the product, what it's utilized for, where to purchase it as well as specifications of the product.

A detailed intro of the product is really crucial, whether it's particular software, website or a video product. Buyers have to know precisely what they're getting before they buy a product.

Describe the functionality of the product. Customers must have a firm understanding of how the product works and under what circumstances.

For instance, if the product is a digital camera, consumers have to know whether or not a camera executes in bad weather, at night or in the harsh sunshine. A digital camera that malfunctions in these sorts of challenges might not be in a buyer's best interest. Same for your video product, you must list how it works.

Describe product features. Readers have to be energized about the possibilities of the product. They need to know what makes the product more beneficial than the rivalry or whether or not it's quicker, more efficient or more user friendly.

For instance, the buyer wants to know if it has better features than other products. They want to know how what subjects are covered and what format is used.

List the product's advantages in order for the buyers to comprehend the benefits of investing in the product. For instance, if the buyer can save time and cash, the value of the product increases or if the product is portable and user friendly, it supplies advantages that may improve the chances of a consumer investing in the product.

To step-up consumer interest, include a list of any extras that will be added to the product. In case of a video product, for instance, a developer might want to include a text version or a free audio only version.

The more a product developer may differentiate his product from like products that are marketed by the rivalry, the greater his chances of drawing in consumers who are willing to invest in it.

Developers must make certain that product info is accurate. Consumers expect to get precisely what the product promises them. Inexact or false info may result in a massive return rate. Exaggerating the features or advantages of a product may leave a permanent stain on the reputation of a developer or organization.

Convince buyers of your credibleness. Before anybody will pay for your video product, they have to be certain it will be money well spent. Describe how you're an authority in the field. Supply comments from other people that have benefited from viewing your videos.

Protect your video. In order to get individuals to pay for your video product, you have to be certain they can't view it for free. Do this by producing a password-protected area of your site and utilizing Clickbank. This may vary based on your Web host, but the selection to password-protect areas of your site are in the control panel.

Send buyers instructions for accessing the video product after they've made a purchase. Once bought, the customer ought to receive an email with the instructions so he or she can view the videos.

Chapter 6:
Final Tips

Synopsis

Nothing is complicated about it. Producing your own video product is indeed that easy. Anybody could do it, in reality. And the applications for this sort of creation are astonishingly diverse.

More Tips

You may add video components to your sales page to step-up your response rate.

Video sales letters are utilized to market products and services in much the same way as traditional marketing copy. They present the viewer with the product being sold, the advantages for purchasing the product, and a call to action in which the viewer is asked to buy the product.

Video sales letters are sensed as effective as they add an element of control to the sales process and intimately mimic the experience of purchasing a product face to face. Many video sales letters utilize either a set of pictures recorded from a computer screen or a live-action video.

Produce a story your target audience may identify with. Successful scripts commonly include stories about an issue and how discovering the product assisted the user in solving the issue. Bring in the main character and the main issue he has to solve.

The story has to clearly define an issue with which your target audience may identify. For instance, your story might be about always losing to your tennis partner by a few points, knowing that the difference was in the backhand and how you carried off consistently out-backhanding him after applying a secret strategy you learned.

Arrive at a list of the features and advantages of the product you want to sell. A feature is something the product has, like 5 hours of training

videos. An advantage is how a certain feature or the product as a whole will better some aspect of the buyer's life.

Arrive at an outline of your video script by blending the story with the features and advantages list.

Edit the script to let in "power words" like "mysterious," "gigantic," and "clockwork" where possible. Power words produce a particular image or feeling for the individual listening to the message. For instance, a prospective buyer is more interested in learning a "mysterious strategy designed to produce gigantic profits daily like clockwork," than a "strategy designed to make you cash daily."

Edit the script so the video duration is 5 to twenty minutes. The length depends upon your target market and the cost of the product. An inexpensive product planned for a buyer with an immediate issue like foot odor calls for less time to convince the individual to purchase.

Utilize your own experience with buying to decide how long to make the video. Equate how much a shop clerk has to say for you to purchase a $1 bar of soap to how long the auto salesman has to convince you to purchase an automobile.

Live Play Video Sales Letters

- Rehearse your script numerous times till it is delivered in a natural and credible way.
- Discover a location and the visual props you require to precisely and effectively express your message.

- Utilize a camcorder to record your video sales letter. This might call for several takes before you're satisfied with the outcome.
- Edit the video utilizing video software to make it appear more professional and to add any particular effects, music or text captions.

Screen Capture Sales Videos

Open up a desktop presentation software package like PowerPoint or Keynote and produce a new project. This is commonly accomplished by selecting "New" from the main menu of many programs.

Produce slides of your video sales script. Break up the script into blocks of text with no more than 4 lines on every slide. Utilize the biggest size font possible to make the text simple to read.

Spotlight the power words in the text in another color than the remainder of the text. Utilize a maximum of 3 colors for your text to avoid confusing the viewer as to which words are more crucial than others.

Utilize a screen-capture program like Camtasia or CamStudio to record the slide show when you read the script to correspond with the text exhibited onscreen. Camtasia is a paid platform and CamStudio is a free platform.

Utilize the video-editing software package included with the screen-capture program to make alterations to the video sales letter.

CamStudio

CamStudio is able to record all screen and audio action on your PC and produce industry-standard AVI video files and utilizing its built-in SWF Producer may turn those AVIs into bandwidth-friendly streaming flash videos (SWFs)

Here are just a couple of ways you are able to utilize this software system:

- You are able to utilize it to produce demonstration videos for any software program
- Or how about producing a set of videos responding to your most often asked questions?
- You are able to produce video tutorials for school or college classes
- You are able to utilize it to produce video-based info products you are able to sell
- You will be able to even utilize it to record new tricks and strategies you discover on your favorite software package, before you forget them!

You may offer downloadable video lessons to step-up consumer confidence.

The Net has made instructional videos more popular than ever. Individuals not only wish to view funny or strange homemade videos online for amusement, but they're likewise seeking instruction for projects around the home or processes to achieve personal business undertakings.

Teachers might want to utilize instructional videos in their courses and businesses utilize videos for training. Observe these tips to make an instructional video of your own.

Begin with planning. Make a storyboard utilizing drawings or photos of what you wish to videotape. Put down the procedures to go along with the images or develop a script.

Utilize any sort of video camera to record as long as you've software and a mic to go with it. Discover that even web cams come with software packages and a sound recording device and a few of them even come with restricted editing capabilities.

Understand you are able to buy a web cam for well under $50 and it commonly comes with specified software.

Review your storyboard and written processes or script prior to shooting. Arrange your props and equipment required. Do a walk-through prior to you actually making an instructional video-rehearse first of all. Go over your lighting; shoot a few preliminary shots to double check your lighting and sound.

Start recording your instructional video recording. Get a volunteer or employ a camera person if you need the camera to be roving or you require 2 cameras (from different angles) on you while you carry out the procedures for your instructional video. Look out for background noises and visual disturbances as well as additional disruptions.

Make certain your steps are clear, exact and understandable for instruction, and viewers may hear and see the processes and step actions well.

Refrain from recording too hot or loud; you are able to always adjust the sound following recording, but don't record too low either. Have a little sound to work with while you finish your video.

Record in scenes or sections if you make an instructional video that's comparatively long. Shoot on a schedule if your video is long and can't be finished in an hour or two. Edit your video if essential if you have an editing software package. Impart effects, scene change artwork and additional enhancements to your video with editing software.

Rather than developing a written manual, you may demonstrate what is needed to be done with a product you're providing through a series of videos that may be packaged together.

Wrapping Up

Selling your digital product with Clickbank is among the best ways to speedily get exposure and sales for your product. Within a couple of business days, you will be able to be up and running and have your product advertized by a huge network of affiliates! Here are the simple steps for getting fixed as a Clickbank vendor:

- Register with Clickbank
- Produce a Pitch Page and Thank You Page
- Create a Payment Link
- Fill out My Site Information inside Your Account
- Fill out My Products Information inside Your Account
- Test Payment Link
- Request Product Approval
- Pay One-Time $49.95 Activation Fee
- You're Finished!

Although Clickbank permits a vast variety of products, there are a few general criteria that all products have to meet. They are:

All products have to be original or suitably licensed, and can't infringe on the intellectual property of other people.

All products have to be delivered to buyers digitally, thru web pages, downloadable files, or e-mail within twenty-four hours of purchase. Immediate delivery is preferable. You must inform the buyer at the time of purchase when they ought to expect product delivery.

You might likewise offer shipped delivery of printed media (for instance books, CDs, and DVDs) to buyers, provided that it's clearly complimentary and not essential to the operation of the original digitally downloaded product.

- Once Clickbank okays your product for sale, it's listed in the Clickbank Marketplace.
- Affiliates on a regular basis search the Marketplace for intriguing fresh products to promote.
- An affiliate comes across your product and decides to market your product. They promote it in many different places online, utilizing an assortment of paid and free promotional strategies, like writing about it on their blog or paying for ads on search engines.
- Their endeavors drive potential buyers to your Pitch Page, where buyers read about your product and decide to purchase.
- After the sale is processed, Clickbank takes its transaction processing consigns (7.5% + $1), then pays the affiliate commission percent (which you decide on) based on the remaining sum. The rest of the cash goes to you. If no affiliate gets the sale, you keep the whole amount following processing charges.

Having affiliates market your product for you may be an enormously profitable way to sell your product, as affiliates bear the burden of ad costs and time. As you only pay out affiliates once a sale actually happens, you don't have to waste any cash on advertising that does not result directly in sales.

www.ingramcontent.com/pod-product-compliance
Lightning Source LLC
Chambersburg PA
CBHW030531220526
45463CB00007B/2784